Dismal Rock

by Davis McCombs

DISMAL ROCK

TUPELO
PRESS

First paperback edition September 2007

Library of Congress Control Number: 2007927239

Tupelo Press, Inc.

PO Box 539, Dorset, Vermont 05251

802.366.8185

tupelopress.org

Cover and text designed by William Kuch, WK Graphic Design

Tupelo Press is an award-winning independent literary press that publishes fine fiction, non-fiction and poetry in books that are as much a joy to hold as they are to read.

Tupelo Press is a registered 501(c)3 non-profit organization and relies on donations to carry out its mission of publishing extraordinary work that may be outside the realm of the large commercial publisher.

We are most grateful to Christopher W. Cronin for contributions to the press that made possible the publication of *Dismal Rock*.

 Supported in part by an award from the
National Endowment for the Arts

For Warren and Charlotte

Acknowledgments

I would like to thank the National Endowment for the Arts and the Kentucky Arts Council for grants that made the writing of this book possible.

I am indebted to the Fulbright College at the University of Arkansas for granting me a Robert C. and Sandra Connor Endowed Faculty Fellowship. I would like to express my gratitude as well to Mr. and Mrs. Connor.

A special thanks to my friend Mark Willis at the U. S. Army Corps of Engineers, without whose detective work and encouragement many of these poems could not have been written. I would also like to thank Rebecca Howell who helped me clarify my thinking about tobacco farming at an early stage in the writing of these poems. Thank you to Colleen and Rick Olson, Bob Cetera, Mr. Dale Huffman and, most of all, to Carolyn.

Grateful acknowledgment is made to the following publications, in which some of these poems were first published:

Alaska Quarterly Review: "A Strange Forbearance," "The Mimic Birds"
Bat City Review: "Fossil Fuel"
Cream City Review: "Northtown Well," "Spider Crystal Descent"
Gulf Stream: "White Space," "Home"
Hayden's Ferry Review: "Fishing At Night"
The Heartland Review: "The Candle"
Insurance: "Ola"
The Kenyon Review: "The Elgin Marbles"
Melee: "Place Names"
The Missouri Review: "Tobacco Mosaic" (winner of the 2005 Larry Levis Editor's Prize)
Pleiades: "Self-Admonition at Summer Seat"
Poetry: "The Mist Netters," "The Last Wolf in Edmonson County"
Tears in the Fence: "Black and Yellow Argiope," "Change of Season," "Lique Log Eclogue"
Virginia Quarterly Review: "Bob Marley" ("Nesta")
Washington Square: "Honeysuckle," "Water Tank Cosmogony"
Willow Springs: "Rossetti in 1869" (winner of the 2005 Vachel Lindsay Poetry Award)
Wind: "Noodling" (winner of the 2005 Joy Bale Boone Poetry Award)
     "Salts Cave Revisited," and very early versions of "Transplants" and "Gnomon" were also first published in the magazine to accompany an interview conducted via email, "A Conversation with Davis McCombs."

"Nineveh" appears in the anthology *Under the Rock Umbrella*, edited by William Walsh, Mercer University Press, 2006.

"Fossil Fuel" appeared in *Missing Mountains: Kentuckians Write Against Mountaintop Removal*, edited by Kristin Johannsen, Bobbie Ann Mason, and Mary Ann Taylor-Hall, Wind Publications, 2005.

"The Elgin Marbles" appeared on Poetry Daily (www.poems.com) on May 19, 2006.

Contents

I

TOBACCO MOSAIC

II

THE MIST NETTERS

TOBACCO MOSAIC

for Mark Willis

The tobacco production technology in use today was originally derived from that used by native people. Tobacco is American.

> —John Van Willigen and Susan C. Eastwood
> *Tobacco Culture: Farming Kentucky's Burley Belt*

Burley Tobacco, as I first knew it, was produced with an intensity of care and a refinement of skill that far exceeded that given to any food crop that I know about. It was a handmade crop; between plant bed and warehouse, every plant, every leaf, was looked at, touched, appraised, lifted, and carried many times. The experience of growing up in a community in which virtually everybody was passionately interested in the quality of the local product was, I now see, a rare privilege.

> —Wendell Berry

Stripping Room

They were working past dark at the waist-high bench
that night; they were smoking and talking in that place
of the barrel stove and of the chalk figures while outside
and all around them, a season folded its leaves
into the ground like wings. They reached their hands
into the veined, elastic plants; they touched the tips
of shadows stretching like fingers from a past
of splintered bone and ash, the dark of the Continent.
Autumn was shifting and rustling, preparing
for sleep, and the moon rose through the empty fields,
flashing its wide search-beam through the roosts.
They were standing at the end of a process, sorting
by the light of jar lamps. In that dust-paneled room,
deep in a dwindling year, they stripped the lugs
and flyings from the stalks and let the bounty
of the long days slip so easily through their hands.

Gnomon

Now deep in thistles and a snarl of broken implements,
the Cross Barn pops its bent nails into the twilight.
He parks the truck by the gate, swings each leg over,
and follows the tilting gravel strip between the silo
and the pond's half-lit disc. A bat is crossing
the water on the boat of its reflection; it is squeaking
like a rusted hinge. Everything he knows there
has been left ajar: the slope of the barn's battered roof,
its wedge of shadow keeping time over the fescue,
even the day around him, even the latticed gloom
of the loading chute where once he waited
for a thunderhead to pass, and felt time rumbling
like a tedder over the fields, each moment flaring up
like a match, consuming itself—all of them scattering
like grasshoppers where the tractor churned the hay.

— apt similies

4

Lexicon

The people are talking about budworms; they are talking
about aphids and thrips. Under the bluff at Dismal Rock,
there where the spillway foams and simmers,
they are fishing and talking about pounds and allotments;
they are saying white burley, lugs and cutters.
Old men are whittling sticks with their pocketknives
and they are saying Paris Green; they speak of topping
and side-dressing; they are whistling and talking
about setters, plant beds and stripping rooms.
At Hedgepeths, under the shade of the Feed Mill awning,
in that place of burlap and seedbins, of metal scoops,
they are sitting on milk crates; they are drinking from bottles
and they are talking about pegs, float plants and tierpoles.
At the Depot Market, they say blue mold, high color;
they are nodding and saying sucker dope; they are leaning
on the counter and talking about Black Patch, high boys, flue-cured.
They are arguing about horn worms and buyouts.
They are saying come back, come back, come back.

Nineveh

That night he camped alone among kudzu and yucca,
pitched the flickering egg of his tent on a shelf of sandstone
above the floodplain, above sinkholes and bottomland,
there where the laurels mesh into a railing, and where
the lights of Munfordville smudge the tree line to the west.
He was drinking bourbon from a plastic cup;
he was listening to a barred owl interrogate the underbrush.
He sat on a stump by the fire while the ridge below him,
that long stone ship, floated on shadow, and he listened
as its cracked hull popped and groaned and sank into the darkness
swirling up from the river, rippling over the low stone decks.
He listened as night swallowed the masts of poplars
and their grapevine rigging, as bats began to pour like grain
out of the empty silos, and the dark kept rising.
The fields were going under one by one. He could see
what he thought was fire on the horizon, smoking
and jumping at the tree line, and he watched until it turned
into the Green Corn Moon, until it climbed the cedar's rungs
out of fog, spilling its light over the town like forgiveness,
over houses, much cattle, and row after row of tobacco.

Nightshade

A freight train crosses between *L* and *N*, its boxcars
rattling on the rails, but the town on the bluff is dreaming
of an enemy soil-borne and legion, of blue mold,
wildfire, brown spot, black shank, rust. It is dreaming
of the sodden, root-sliced dark where they bide their time.
A moth bumps a yellow porchlight, beats ripples
in the hot air, and the dreams of the town, as if to snare it,
float like a spider's casting strand toward street lamps,
past a billboard's flood-lit lettering and over the line
where sawbriars turn to cedars and the slopes fall off
to river bottoms, soggy and damp. An owl will glide unseen
up prong-horned sloughs tonight, but the thoughts
of the sleeping people drift, untethered, toward leaf undersides
and stem cores, that vowel-haunted dark where the blight
that stalks the stalks all summer girds itself and grows strong.

Tobacco Culture

Then came that moment when they thought again of the river.
Looking up from their work, they thought of fishing there,
of prowling the charred rock shelters on its banks.
They thought of sunlight, still warm and splattering
on the mossy stones, and it pulled them from the fields of stobs,
from the barn's hot tierpoles; it pulled them from the burley,
housed and curing, and they disappeared down cowpaths
at the edge of fields; they slid through stingweed
and the sycamores scabbed with lichen. They carried tackleboxes;
they carried canes; they carried flashlights; the young boy
on the path gripped a flashlight, and its beam was a filament
that reeled him through the gloom of the sloping overhang,
pulling him, step by wobbling step, toward the shelf of stone
above the flood-line and the pipe carved out of banded slate
that was waiting for him there, waiting for centuries in dust
and in the scent of nicotine still clinging to the ash caked in its bowl.

Liming the Patch

They had taken a spud and worked the gravestones out
of their sockets. In that dim room, where pipesmoke vined
wallpaper roses and yellowed the lamp's rickety shade,
he could almost hear the shuffle and scrape of their tools
as she talked. *It was shameful*, she told him, *what they done.*
He could picture them waiting until dusk to approach
the clump of walnuts circling the old graveyard.
They had waited until the gray light there masked their faces.
They had taken every stone: the polished blocks, the little
scratched and unmarked chunks on the perimeter—all
had been hoisted onto the flatbed wagon. *It wasn't right.*
Two men with a crusher came. He could see the gullies
of the white-powdered fields, the deep unlettered dirt.
She talked and the lampshade sputtered, wind nudged
the walnuts, and August baked the new moon's mud into a brick.

Bat Gaddie and the Centennial Exposition

Just beyond and through this, a wind was rumpling
the old man's clothes, touching his face, or threading
the grass of the sloped field where he walked.
It was the beginning of winter. He felt it in the broomsticks
of his legs; he felt it in the split hoehandles of his arms.
He entered from the north gate and crows, scattering off
in threes, called his name, or something not unlike it,
from the barn and from the creekline where minnows
flashed across the leaf-stained water. The corncrib cranked
its shadow over the fenceposts, and he thought of sunlight
splotching the rock shelves at water level. He thought
of the hogshead of leaves he wrestled up the ramp
and onto the train in Bonnieville, of the hands, unknown to him,
that would unpack the cask. He thought of flanges and pistons,
their music humming as it faded over cross-tied iron rails.

Transplants

The young man walks where Bat once walked, over
the same tilting slope, the creek in the distance flashing
its signal mirror through gaps in the trees, its windblown
rustle of water and moss. He straddles gullies
at the red-clay edge of fields, stumbles, and though he walks
in sunlight, he knows that in the mesh of leaves beside him,
under the hornworm's path, a mortuary darkness waits.
A hard rain shreds the afternoon's clumped heat; it drips
off the ribs of the drooping leaves; it pushes potsherds
through the sediment, mixing and sorting what the plow reveals,
dispersing flint chips and projectiles, disarticulating bone
from bone. Now comes the wind off the bottomland;
it enters in the wake of the storm; it sniffs at the dirt-
splattered stalks, and smudges the downpour's tracks
while the man is sleeping. Of this much he is certain:
the roots in the long rows suture the furrows; in the kiln
of summer, even the hoed earth scabs like a wound.

Smoke

Under the bluffs and ridges, under the ponds and barrens,
under the fields of yellowing leaf, the cave hoards its trove
of corridors. A man is walking there with a cane torch;
he is stooping with a greaselamp, crouching with a Bengal Light;
a boy is climbing with a lantern (coal-oil, now Coleman); now
a woman is crawling with carbide, chimneying up a shaft
with halogen; she is canyon-walking in the glow of a light-
emitting diode. At Bedquilt, Austin, at New Discovery: there,
where the hills' flanks crumble and the hands of undergrowth cup
the entrances' dark flames, visitations come; from Colossal
and Salts, fragments and emissaries arrive on the wind
from other worlds. *Tobacco*, the old man said, *is a holy spirit*
with great medicine, but abuse it, and its power will kill you.

Hobart

He clucked his tongue, slapped the bull's rump, and turned
a herd of Angus, single file, through the narrow gap
in the fence to the barn lot. He lingered by the tailgate
of his pickup, smoked while the sky reeled icy cirrus
over the fescue, and foretold the sheets of rain that, by mid-
week, draped the blue hills and approached, the hay bales
safe in the loft. He played the barn vents at curing time
like the stops of an instrument, and went on, cupping
his hands around the life he'd inherited as if it were a flame.
The cedars smoked their pollen into the blue air; a drought month
lit the shucks of fall, and he searched the sky's empty bowl
but never saw the storm that, far beyond him, was purpling
like a bruise and taking everything he took for granted.

Nicotiana

Tobacco, he was told, *paid for your education* and all along the bluff
that afternoon, grasshoppers sprang up from his footsteps
and shook faint ripples through the amethyst air of late July.
He stumbled down a slope of fescue, through sawbriars
and the mesh of the tree line; he entered the weedbeds
at the water's crumpling edge; he entered the creek,
that plane of sliding liquid, and he stepped over rocks
that split and swiveled it. He has not forgotten that day.
He has sat alone at a table and thought of it. Rubbing the sticks
in his hands together, he has wanted to rekindle its fire.
He thinks of the stones sunk deep in their sockets of mud;
he thinks of stretching his legs, of crossing to the other bank.
He thinks of the words he writes, of the dark like silt
beneath them, and of the secret hiding like a crayfish there.

Drought

Now the river hones its dull blade on a strop of gravel,
and the bobcats, sensing this, come down off the dry
ridgetops, slake their thirst at the water's sharpened edge,
and cling to the shade of bank-side undergrowth.
This is the time of the brick kiln, of pond craters,
that month when even moonlight chars the limp cornsilks
in the fields. Now the people come, the men stripping
shirtless in pokeweed and pawpaws; they come
to where the riffles' flashbulbs strobe the sycamores,
to the still pools above the Railroad Bridge where carp mope
and algae bloom. The children paddle out in inner tubes,
they hide a watermelon at the Blue Hole. At dusk,
their parents build great fires of driftwood on the gravel,
roasting hotdogs on willow prongs. They crank the handle
of the ice cream churn, mopping their foreheads,
and celebrate, though their hearts are burning, and the leaves
on the blue hills high above them vanish into smoke.

Rain Dog

It is raining in Hart County: a thunderhead has pinned
its flapping sheets along the Interstate; big blood-warm drops
are rattling through gutters, strumming the high-tension wires.
At Pine Ridge Hill, Glen Lily, at Hundred Acre Pond,
runnels knit, loosen quartzite from conglomerate,
and push the clattering gravel waves down gullies,
through sinkholes, pouring them into vertical shafts
toward the water table. Run-off is scarring the topsoil.
It is undermining the pilings of a wooden footbridge.
Along the shelf of the Escarpment, trickles thicken
into torrents; seeps unlock and scour the outcrops,
depositing tufa. Taps and spigots in the bluffs
beside the river start to drip. Even in the new subdivision,
rain is buckling the freshly laid sod, frothing through
storm drains by the curb, rinsing the lost dog's world of its map.

The Tobacco Economy

This is the burley-curing heat of autumn, a light
like the sweat-burnished grain of pegs; this
is the green truck's unlatched vent and the full moon
rippling on the warehouse roof; this is the river's
whorled thumbprint, the water's surface dark as ink.
This is the shell mound and the cover crop, the soaked
dirt gullies of the tilting road; this is the clank
of a hoe's metal blade and the notched flint prototype
it struck; this is the deep tobacco row; this is the humming,
strained and constant, of the feedstore's window unit,
the worm-riddled posts of the boundary fence,
and the eye-watering air of the vented barn. He stands,
it seems, downwind of a smoldering heap, and these
are what float back to him like ash flakes crackling with fire.

The Sharecroppers

So many moons have risen through the fields of leaf.
So many suns have turned the rows of stobs to cover crops
and turned away: it sank like a stain into the hills that night,
a flash, without heat, on the dust-coated window
of the stripping room and the unlit barrel stove inside.
On that day of the developers and the divvying up,
he walked the farm and thought of those who labored there.
He crouched in the shade of the barn, thinking and mumbling,
and the wind ripped the words from his mouth, spun them
along an edge of sheering air. He thought of someone
in a barn or field far away looking up to see who spoke;
he thought how nothing he could ever say would match
the sound of the undergrowth's inquietude that last night
when barred owls talked in the timbered sink, and he heard
in the call of the towhee the sound of the end of the world.

THE MIST NETTERS

Rossetti in 1869

He'd walk for miles, they said, to pluck a strand
of colored ribbon from a robbin's nest
and pocket it. Once, Rossetti watched the moon's
reflection in a hoofprint full of water
on the road, and even in London
they'd told the story of how, despite the dark,
despite the rain, he'd stood transfixed for hours.

In his absence from Tudor House, the rumor
swirled, but only he knew what he'd seen there:
a way of painting that might shrink the distance
between brush stroke and object—*this* reflection,
that moon, and not the scumble of pigments
he applied to canvas and called a lily
or Venetian glass. Only he knew how, for months,

he'd seen his dead wife everywhere. Hoofbeats…
He watched the moon's reflection in the puddle blur
as the horseman, startled at finding him lampless
and disheveled on a drizzling night, slowed to a canter.
Canter, Rossetti thought, *for Canterbury,
the pilgrims' loping gate.* He gathered his greatcoat
about him and walked on in the rain.

Seven years, he thought, and yet in seven more
how many times will snow come scurrying
through the wrought-iron fence at Highgate?
Seven Springs have plunged their swords of thaw

into the ground; seven Autumns dragging their cloaks
of leaves across the cracked earth of her grave.
Each season, in its turn, obliterates.

That summer he'd found a wounded chaffinch
on the road and carried it to Penkill Castle
in the pocket of his coat, a tiny bird,
toppled from its attic of wind, that came,
as he walked, to stand for all her suffering.
Sometimes he could almost hear the tinkling
of plates and glasses from that long-dead night:

neuralgia, laudanum, the miscalculated dose.
She had known his infidelities. Now she lay
beneath wild asparagus and dandelions—
dent de lion, its pointed petals like a great cat's tooth—
but it was the poems, his only copy, braided
in her long red hair, that obsessed him,
that had driven him to Girvan, a holiday

that by all accounts had been disastrous:
nothing would silence the frogs, nothing
would bring his own words back into his mind.
*Fiasco, Italian for common flask, the glassblower's
mistake.* What words he could remember
came to him now with the taste of distant lands
or long-dead languages—the stale, held breath of crypts.

How easily as a child he'd moved from the Italian
of his parents to the Greek and Latin of school,
and through the streets of London blowing

with the drift of English across trade routes
and continents. With the snap of a broadsail,
words arrived like stowaways from other tongues
and passed, anonymous, into the leaf-swirl and traffic.

That night he dreamed of running, a forest
full of smoking stumps. He woke in the dark
and waited until dawn creaked open like a trunk
of light, its widening lid of clouds at the horizon.
He threw himself into the horse's
lathering neck and home toward Chelsea:
his garden at Tudor House, the wombat,

the camel, the room full of armor…
and Highgate waiting in the mist and ink
of night. Bonfire, *bone fire*, a light that flickers
and falls on splintered roots and clay.
He knew at last what he must do: his hands
remembering the shank of a spade, remembering
a hole in the ground where the dark exhales.

Fishing at Night

As if what waited
in the dark
were different
than what travelled
through it: a chalk
moon rose and filled
the fossil beds
with light. Print
of a crinoid,
print of a shell.
Here at the slate bar's
end, where water
swirls and eddies,
I worked the bait
into the dark, bent
my concentration
to its snags and cur-
rent, the line
going taut then
slack. It wasn't
so much the river
as it clucked
and settled over eggs
of chert, but how
it hatched itself
years deeper
in its groove,
how it whispered
obsolescence

with each cleaned hook,
my own veins
pressed like fish scales
in a sunless,
uncracked rock
or book.

Water Tank Cosmogony

The leaves that sank to its bottom
were not magnified by the trembling
of the liquid, nor its stillness, nor
its bevel at the corrugated rim.
A season decanted where a bullfrog
drummed his throat to the black gnats
strafing the watery lens—but how,
across that long drought summer
when we sold the herd, through fields
of parched, uneaten pasture, did he hear
its oval note of rain and aluminum?
I would have turned the valve that night
and let the water flow, a rippling plane,
into the grass, but I just stood there,
frozen like the frog in the beam
of my flashlight, while the deep grass
roar of summer pulsed around us,
and a meteor swam, I swear,
like a tadpole though the glistening dark.

Old Munford Inn

Hart County Civil War Days
Munfordville, Kentucky

Are words more beautiful than things? That night
a flecked moth tried the window's rusty screen,
clicking and clicking, and for a time it seemed
our voices, mingling at the punchbowl's rim,
might summon those who knew the answer.
We spoke the syllables that stand in
for the dead, and I hoped they would be drawn,
faint and improbable, to the circle of refracted light.
Outside, the boxwoods lobbed their shadows
on the grass; the galaxy flowed west across
the bridge's empty pilings. No one who knew
came back to us, not those from under
the iron bootscrape rusting, not the man unwound
from the river's sheets, nor even Sarah, *Sometime Slave*
Always Our Friend, from her stone on Craddock Hill.

The Mist Netters

They stretched their web between two poplars
and across the cave mouth while dusk seeped
insatiably toward them, but now it's dark,
and they are fidgeting with tripods, headlamps,
packs stuffed full of gear. Crouched on a rock,
I watch them trample through the ecotone
in lug boots, test flash strobes on the net.
Every year this exit count, a yield
of raw data in a spiral notebook jotted down
by lantern light. Every year the hush that falls
until, like a splatter of rain, the first bats hurtle
into the hair-thin fibers. Only the vaccinated
can come near enough to disentangle wings, claws,
and fit selected species with tiny transistors.
Up close, the bats are struggling, scrunch-faced.
They aren't— am I alone in suspecting this?—
bats until we see them, nor afterwards,
when banded and released, they flop out
past the lantern's scorch of light, past
our radio telemetry and over the visible
prongs of branches that tonight are tuning forks
the leaves reach out to touch and silence.

Black and Yellow Argiope

The spider by the compost bin
is trawling the warm air currents
off the creek with his net tonight.

He is far out to sea.
My flashlight on the dumped
eggshells, coffee grounds,

and rinds is the last beacon
he will sight
before dawn appears

like a landfall of far blue hills
that crest and disappear
and grow closer. He must

content himself with each
day's catch of gnats and midges
(it is enough) but surely

he is waiting for the night
that may never come
when a dragonfly

swimming low and fast
from the shadowy
banks and moss

mistakes his grid of strands
for a ripple in the air
and does not swerve.

Honeysuckle

> Our bodies every seven years are completely fresh-
> materiald—seven years ago it was not this hand that clench'd
> itself against Hammond.
> > —John Keats, Letter to the George Keatses in Kentucky
> > September 1819

Coyotes are passing swift and scratchless up the mud-dark sloughs
        tonight; incorporeal
they call to us from the sawbriars, discarnate they yelp
        at the moon reflected
on the river's wrinkling skin. Daddy flicks a cigarette from the bed
        of the truck, its arc
like our own through the darkening, bodiless air.
        We travel, it seems,
away from the still-lit portion of the field or something like it,
        flutter like moths
toward the shadow the barn casts or, to put it simply, the fencerows
        are blooming again.
A week? Two? The honeysuckle bares its dripping fangs
        to the barbed wire.
What is the element that fills the spaces we vacate, that trembles
        like a wall of water
barring the way back? This scent of boundaries and incursions
        that rises with the warm air
off the river comes, as I do, from a source in the knotted spring.
        I stray
from the tail-lights' bitter glow to the woodline; though dark,
        it opens
into sun-speckled leaves. I press my face into the night and toward
        a distant field,
unreachable now, a face in the weeds that was mine, a sturdy little body
        breaking into light.

Bob Marley

Jamaica, 1996

The storm's first bullets pit the sand
this side of the wrinkling wave-line; the island,

as I remember it, drums in rain, a barefoot
beach guard hurrying beneath a sheet

of corrugated tin, or the light that followed,
a blush of watery blues and yellows

that drained off past the ocean's rim. We stalked
the grounds of Point Village: the cobbled walks,

a bonfire smoldering on the bulwark, the tree frog
we never saw but heard above the bug-

filled racket—and that was all I'd known of you,
I thought, a voice like weeping where bamboo

clacked in wind, a wisp of smoke,
torchlight dappling the jetty's granite blocks.

In Negril we were duped and hustled
for a week, but even there, in the muscled,

blood-veined face of the bauxite mine,
in the coconuts we drank with straws—too green,

lobotomized—something more, some quiver
of a man, of fingers at the strings of your guitar.

You were there in the musk and bustle of the market:
a smell of curried goat, the skin on a bullet-

wood drum, there, later, when the storm spread
like a bruise along the coast, dark clouds

scudding across the smoke-gray chop
of the horizon; I watched a line of raindrops

run the ribs of a palm frond, a far hill suffused
with light. And then came news

of the water strike, week-long and island-wide,
the stench of the backed-up commode.

I have waited too long to credit the flesh,
have hated its inconstancy, how it hastens into ash

and dust, and so I almost missed the Doctor Bird
that day at Tangle River, the way it hovered

above the red bromeliad, dipped its needle beak
into each blossom, and seemed to pluck

the air—before it vanished in the bush—
into a string that shivered through and shook us.

What Floyd Said

A late wind scuffs the water of the pond
and you will look for me there,
for what, if anything, survives
the glass-topped coffin or the looted grave.

It's not that I might still endure, mud-
plastered in the glow of a single bulb
that scares you; it's the possibility
that I don't. No, that *you* won't.

That night you saw the figure of a man
carved in shadow by the taillight,
the tip of a cigarette quickly
extinguished, and gasped my name.

Do you think I shuffle, mumbling,
down a gravel road at dusk,
or that I linger in the grip
of some damp rat-hole still? Do you?

The wagon lurched into the dark
and the moment vanished. Even
the cave in its nest of undergrowth
cries with an open beak to be fed.

You know this. Think of the Entrance
as it is tonight, how the bats at twilight
will ascend black ropes of water
unraveling toward the mossy slabs.

Look for me there at your peril,
for a year played into a shallow grave
by the crickets' tuneless fiddling:
a sound like a season wasting its breath.

Local Color

In the early 1950's, William Logan of Brownsville
invented and briefly sold a paint made from the
county's abundant natural asphalt. He called it
Loganite Ventrasuvius Paint.

—*A History of Edmonson County, Kentucky*

And sure enough, a thick, obliterating snow
erased the crack on Dismal Rock; it hurried
through the trees at Cedar Sink, and settled
into humps on the cold gravestones at Joppa.
That night the moon pried open the ridge's lid
and climbed the poplars, and if, through its branch-
marbled light, Bill Logan's ghost came stumbling,
if he found the spot where his lab once stood,
and set to work mixing pigments in a crock,
it was because the snow knows the future,
because the hours between the fox's footfall crunch
and dawn were cut down by a light that, blue
and heatless, sketched in the frosted hills
and found him there, alone in a glittering field.

Noodling

If he thinks of them even once, the focus
of his gaze will ripple, and so he nodded,
pushed past them off the boatramp where
they arced their spinning lures, and entered
the river's inelastic bands of current.
He finds himself neck-deep and swaddled,
the river smearing a poultice of mud
and rotting leaves over the veins in his feet.
He finds himself out past the reach of water-
beaded lines, of hooks and sparkling hope,
the shallows swiveling around him.
In his wrists the pulse of unlit rivers throbs,
a hundred million years of water,
but he is picturing a catfish, holed up
and fanning its eggs, a hollow log.
Where he stands, light flecks the surface,
currents, soft-mouthed, suck at hooks
and nuzzle past his shins. He is not afraid,
not now, though he goes with no tackle, no bait,
his mud-gloved fingers wiggling in the murk.
He holds his breath for a muskie's lunge,
a snake bite, a snapping turtle, a gar...
but he is waiting for the moment
when a bolt of iridescence might slither
through his hands, for the instant, instantly lost,
before he'll flip it, thrashing, on the bank.

Salts Cave Revisited

Sir I have found one of the Grat wonder of the world in this cave
Which is a muma
Can All Seed hear after found March the 8
1875
T.E. lee J.L. lee an W.d. Cutliff dicuvers

—*"The Discovery Stone," Salts Cave*

I.

Her breath in the beams
of our headlamps plumed
like smoke that night
at Mummy Valley,
and it was there, sprawled
on the dust-covered slab
in front of us, that she told
at last the story of a bluff
encampment and of the boy
who, darkly and long ago,
stepped from his nine cramped
years into the trickling,
bat-swarmed cup
of Salts Cave sink alone.
In that dim vestibule,
in rats' nests and alluvium,
he lit a clump of Solidago
stalks and slipped into a world
where light, like water,
was a thing he carried,

a desert of shadows
that forked and lengthened
and somewhere—the turns
of the way back still
unspooling in his mind—
a misstep, a rock dislodged,
some lost event that snapped
the thread and brought him,
bruised and hemorrhaging,
to the ledge above us
where two thousand
years later, Bill Cutliff lifted
his coal-oil lamp and gasped.

II.

There were nights that fall
when the lamp on my desk
could have been the only light
in the world. I took it,
hand-cupped and globeless,
down a mossy slump of rocks,
past bats whirling like ash
from the horizontal flue
of a cave: I was following
Bill Cutliff, Tom and John
Lee, their bootprints
and a whiff of acetylene
far ahead, and I went searching,
as they did, for the jolt
that might come once

in a life or not at all,
for a fetal, desiccated thing
still recognizable
as a little boy so near
and so far from home.

Home

Near where the windmill cranked its shadow
on the grass, a bee was scribbling over
trumpet vine on the barn's side, crossing it out;
a moth as big as the boy's dusty hand
pressed its wings into a plank and disappeared,
and the gap-toothed disc kept turning, turning.

It was like that: a peacock roosting on the chimney
of the house, cats in the breezeway, a shelf
of books, and distantly, a freight train screeched
and threw a slash of sparks into the brush
and bent iron tracks before the bridge—all true.

Less so, there was a road and one spring night,
years ago, when glowworms lit the right-of-ways
like exit lights and that same boy, walking there
with a stick, whacked at weeds and hummed
a little wobbly tune that was almost, even then, a wheel.

Fossil Fuel

We found cars and semis burrowing
the air up the hill's steep grade,
wind off their grilles and mudflaps
dragging snow in bands
over the pitted asphalt, but not
the Trilobites we'd come for.
I thought of sleeping in a bed
of shale, undisturbed by the chisel's
sulfurous clank or the seams
of moisture that, freezing, wedge
the bluff's cracked joints apart.
A hammer, a roadcut, a tourniquet
of vines: we didn't find a thing
worth taking. The day picked
the flesh off the hill's white bone,
tightened its talons of sleet
on the rock. I hunched my back
to the wind and wintry mix, shivered
in my thick coat, and set my face
toward a temple built in air:
that great downshifting wake
of traffic that would leave,
I knew, not one stone upon a stone.

Lique Log Eclogue

for Milton and Warren McCombs

A smoking ditch of frogs, the racket of an owl—
he passed the rain-bleached shell of a box turtle
on a rock as he climbed the ridge.
He was near home now; he knew that much,
and he walked on, certain at times of the way,
at times less certain (it was little more
than a cowpath and it was almost dark),
the sloped bluffs falling to his right and left
and suddenly, something: a shiver in the air,
two notes, silence—and there it was again:
Maude, he knew this time, calling his name
from the back porch steps and across
the darkness that thickened between them.
He fished a pipe from his pocket, struck
a match, and in that hand-cupped flare
the scene around him shook and faltered:
the stumps and outcrops, his own feet
not two yards from the edge of Turnhole Sink,
from sandstone and grapevines plunging
out of sight. He answered her, turned around
and walked home to the faces waiting for him
there, and the darkness thickened, Warren,
it thickens to the lightless coal-oil flame
the past burns up in, to the smoke-blue tint
of Joppa Ridge in the still audible distance, or this
echo from its fog-slumped, crumbling base—
a Bobwhite? a Barred Owl?—two notes
of the sound that might lead you there.

43

Spider Crystal Descent

for Charles Wright

These were the cave mouths
summer caught and wrapped
in its strands; these were
our points of entry and departure.

That night, by flash-lit topo map
and compass, we found a set
of thatched coordinates, a dark heart
fluttering in a web. Then others:

Crystal, Bedquilt, Woodson-Adair,
those breathing limestone vents
spun furiously in roots and vines
by a season powerless to snare them.

They wait there still, where shadowed
branches grid; they wait,
bat-hung, crumbling,
the beams of our headlamps

long extinguished, the summer
narcotized, sucked dry and scattered:
grain of the night sky's empty hour-
glass, bow of the fiddlehead fern.

The Elgin Marbles

When Elgin contemplates
    the marbles
now, though for half a century
        they have rested
under glass amid the soot
        streams and traffic

of London, he will see them,
        more often
than not, as under water,
        distorted
by a lens that, though it wobbles
        and shifts,

betrays no sign of how the ship
        that bore them
foundered on a stretch of rocky
        coast, how the teak-
wood planks of the hull had snapped
        and splintered

and how the metopes and stellae
        slid
from their crates of packing
        straw, slipped
the pleats of waves, and hit the soft
        sand floor

of the Aegean with a thud.
      It is 1841,
the light from the stone-
      mullioned
windows of Broomhall House
      is amber,

mid-century, dying. Nothing
      remains
of the fortunes squandered on salvage,
      the rumors
of forgery that dogged the exhibition.
      Old now, near

death, Elgin remembers the blue salt water
      where the marbles
sank—thoughts that will shake him
      like a flame,
as some forty years earlier
      torchlight

guttered and fell upon the white,
      Pentelic
marble columns of the Narthex.
      In that faltering light,
Don Giovanni Battista Lusieri,
      under orders

from the Ambassador himself,
      surveys
the scaffolding, and noting
      with alarm

the lateness of the hour,
                    summons

his draftsmen to the wind-
                    lass cordage.
At his signal the sawed-up pieces
                    of the outer
frieze are lowered, one
                    by one,

down the ramp of the Acropolis.
            Dawn begins to stir
in Attica, just as one cumbersome
            chunk of marble
slips from the sling and shatters
            in a spray of chalk

and thunder. *I was obliged,*
            he wrote to Elgin,
to be a little barbarous. It is one more
            in a series
of ill portents: the owl that, gray-eyed,
            watched

the masons from her bulk of sticks
            in the pediment,
the tremors that have shaken
            and jerked
the city for a month, and now
            this. The faces
of the Janissary guards remain
            as cold

and inscrutable as ever, but from
              this moment,
the intervening years begin
              to bank

and roll like clouds; the sun-
              light
seeping through them rises
              on the slopes
of the Acropolis, on the bones
              of the Parthenon

that each day color from blue
              to ochre
to the blinding white of noon.
              What sculptures
remain in Athens weather to a low-
              relief.

And though the same sun
              that throws
its shadows down the length
              of the frieze
will hover at the treeline until
              nearly dawn,

it is night in Scotland, where Elgin,
              exiled to the remnants
of his own ancestral home, labors
              to breathe.

In the British Museum, once
        or twice

each night, like a ray of sunlight
        refracted
through water, the beam
        of the watch-
man's lamp will cross the marbles.
        By day it is

the faces of the population
        that shimmer
and fade from the glass. Some, more
        than others,
will linger before the musculature
        of the figures,

before their life-like arms and torsos,
        to catch the faintest
spittle of sea in the air, the scent
        of Greece
that is the scent of dry-rust and basil,
        or the bruised,

collective breath of its tombs
        that on a swirling
Autumn day in 1817, in the middle
        of England, rose
from the muted stones to ruffle the auburn
        hair of Keats.

A Strange Forbearance

There were nights when the fire he'd light
at the pond's rim hissed and recoiled,
as if whatever stalked its withering edge
drew close: sparks and the galaxy's botched erasure,
snow dropping off a branch. He'd think
of his children then, asleep in their beds,
how their soft breath, when he tucked them in,
fogged the mirror his face made in theirs.
Who's there? He'd crunch his stick in the coals.
What's out there? and though nothing
ever answered, he'd know by the click of wind
in the black oaks, by the restlessness of snow,
that something was near, that only
by its strange forbearance was he kept there
staring into the flames while the hunch
of a figure took shape at his back, a face
roughed out by the firelight's glittering ax.

The Mimic Birds

To survive like the song
of some lost species
in the throats
of the mimic birds—
a sequence of notes
in the call of a jay,
a snatch of
a mockingbird's
vast repertoire—
to live on like that
as something half-
remembered and
passed down was
all the afterlife
he could allow
himself to hope for:
a voice thrown
into a stone where
it stayed, a phrase,
a figment, dis-
embodied and residual,
among the bluffs
and trees he sang
of, haunted.

Northtown Well

This is the mossed and mortared shade
that steadied them; this is the circle of stone.
They let down ropes into the aquifer
and gaped like children toward a dark,
unspooling liquid. There was a caprock
and a windlass; there were gravestones
on the hill's cracked skull, a church's
hulking shadow. An owl might wait
all day unnoticed in the underbrush; quail
might startle at nightfall from the tall grass
where a man once paced with a willow
fork that bobbed and shuddered.
There were chinks in the transmigration.
He said *here* and the town's slim taproot
formed a wick to water, *here*
and faces like the ones that wobbled up
on buckets bent and were quenched.

White Space

All day snow fell on the river like thistledown,
sowing its spiked seeds into the trough
between the bank where a crow stopped squawking
and the bank where there was silence,
and the wind in the middle moaning like a low fire.
How to say it? How to get it in edgewise?
I walked out hours later under a night sky clouds
were fading from like breath from a lens,
its ground and polished depth becoming
visible, and there, low at the treeline, a squinting,
yellow eye, not answering but watching.

Place Names

That was the winter of Eminent Domain: a porch collapsing
from the weight of no footsteps, a gravestone vanishing
in underbrush. Twelve miles and half a century down
the chip-and-gravel road from our farm, a man said *Joppa*
meaning church, his store, the house, a garden: *Joppa*
until nothing was left but wind in the cedars, a name
frozen to a map. Who is left to speak of what this was?

Here, beyond the boundaries of the Park, words still
take root on outcrops, ponds, boundary oaks, and barns;
they drop like seeds from the birds that land on barbed wire,
one by one, until the fenceline is a treeline, a weave
and cross-hatch of twigs and thickened light and sound.

Tonight, the year's first dust of snow started falling on the road
past Mansfield Bend, and as I drove, it fell on Summer Seat,
Paul Wheeler's Barn, and Haunted Hill. It fell, no doubt,
on Woodsonville and darkly on the spine of Dismal Rock.

The Candle

And then a scene, sketched, as if in pencil,
by the twilight's unsteady hand: mud of an undercut
creek bank, an outcrop of stone across which
has fallen the spindle of a poplar snapped by wind.
It is early spring; a bulb of gnats flickers on
above the damp leaves. In the foreground
a boy approaches through sawbriars the stump
where the tree broke off. It rises like a lectern
from a clump at its base of what may be bloodroot.
He cannot believe what he sees there: a candle
is burning in a circle of pebbles on the moss.
The woods are empty. It is early still.

Self-Admonition at Summer Seat

Consider the shelf of cracked bedrock where the roots
of cedars knuckle down. Knuckle down.
Think of the trees as flames that burn all winter
and warm no one, their roots like wicks
into the oily dark, their branches sputtering
in a gust of starlings. Remember the mounds
and sockets of the old graveyard, the murderous
crows on the hill that shout into the coming night
and eye you hungrily. Imagine the rabbit
that will skitter at nightfall from its den to the base
of the hill, the coyote crouching there. Be silent
before the scuffles and blood they will print in snow.
Let the wind move its hands across the field's
blank page without you, while dusk, coming early now,
inks the treeline's smoldering arch as you write.

The Last Wolf in Edmonson County

Then I stood below the pedestal of Dismal Rock
as shadows straggled up like sheep from the river.
I wanted to believe his ghost might prowl among them,
that something of his hunger might still be limping
down a faint scent trail to its end, but I could not.
Autumn lit the wicks of the leaves; the river, foaming,
garbled, recovered its voice. I did not climb
the flash-lit, switchback trail to the rockhouse.
I did not stand before the petroglyphs again
nor rake at the midden of ash below them with a stick.
I waited until the dark took everything
but the sound of water: the spillway's troughs of stone,
the dam's thick plug. I waited where the blood-spoor
of local narrative intersects a trail gone cold,
and what came stalking there was not a shade, though
it moved with stealth among the sawbriars, lit by nothing.

Ola

Joppa Churchyard
M. M. 1915-1917

—egg-shaped, barely
consonantal. The road
hairpins and plunges,
but I can't stop myself
from stopping here:
sandstone, cedars,
the building's tilt
its eventual undoing.
Where are the things
you touched? Sunlight
through the toppling
chimney stones, a clump
of daffodils. Flute
note, bottle, breath
in a bone. You
matter. You still matter.

Notes

Dismal Rock is a cracked sandstone outcrop almost two hundred feet high located on the east bank of the Nolin River in Edmonson County, Kentucky. On its surface can be found prehistoric petroglyphs dating back several thousand years.

I. Tobacco Mosaic (pp. 3-18)

Tobacco Mosaic is a disease affecting plants of the tobacco family.

The form of these poems was suggested to me by Les Murray's magnificent "The Buladelah-Taree Holiday Song Cycle."

I consulted a number of sources during the writing of these poems. *Tobacco Culture* by John Van Willigen and Susan C. Eastwood and *Kentucky Tobacco Patch* by Virgil Steed were particularly helpful.

Bat Gaddie and the Centennial Expsosition (p. 10)
Bartholomew Bennett (Bat) Gaddie was my great-great-great grandfather. He was born in 1835 and lived in the county in Kentucky where I grew up. By the turn of the twentieth century, he was considered one of the finest growers of burley tobacco in the state and was commissioned by the government in Frankfort to send a hogshead of his best tobacco to the Centennial Exposition in St. Louis.

Smoke (p. 12)
I took the phrase, "fragments and emissaries" from *Journey to the Ants* by Bert Holldobler and Edward O. Wilson. A debt also to *Tobacco Use by Native North Americans: Sacred Smoke and Silent Killer*, edited by Joseph C. Winter.

Nicotiana (p. 14)

Several years ago, my lifelong friend and fellow Park Ranger and writer
Tres Seymour showed me a poem he'd written called "Nicotiana." I stole
his title.

II. The Mist Netters (pp. 21-58)

"Rossetti in 1869" (p. 21)

I wrote the first draft of this poem in the coffee shop of a Borders bookstore
in Palo Alto, California in the spring of 1998. At that time, I consulted
a number of books on etymology and at least one book on Rossetti's
paintings. I regret that I cannot more fully acknowledge my debt to them.

"What Floyd Said" (p. 34)

In 1925, Floyd Collins was trapped and died in Sand Cave, Kentucky.

"Noodling" (p. 37)

Also called grabbling, tickling, hogging or dogging, noodling is the sport of
fishing for large catfish by hand.

"The Elgin Marbles" (p. 45)

I consulted *The Elgin Marbles* by Christopher Hitchens in the writing of
this poem.

"The Last Wolf in Edmonson County" (p. 57)

On January 16, 1902, a man named Noah Duvall shot and killed the last
wolf in Edmonson County, Kentucky, between Bylew and Briar Creek,
near the base of Dismal Rock.